A Guide To Child Support In New Jersey

Bari Zell Weinberger, Esq.

FAMILY LAW REFERENCE COLLECTION
Weinberger Law Group

Weinberger Law Group Library
119 Cherry Hill Road, Suite 120
Parsippany, NJ 07054

www.weinbergerlawgroup.com

ISBN- 978-1-942725-05-3

A Guide To Child Support In New Jersey

Table of Contents

About The Author

Bari Z. Weinberger, Esq. is a certified matrimonial law attorney and founding partner of Weinberger Law Group. With offices located throughout New Jersey, Weinberger Law Group is New Jersey's largest law firm dedicated solely to divorce and family law. In addition to working with clients, Ms. Weinberger is the Associate Author of the New Jersey Family Law Practice, 15th Ed., a 5-volume treatise utilized by virtually every family law judge and practitioner in the State of New Jersey.

Disclaimer

This book provides a general overview of New Jersey divorce and family law matters for informational purposes only. The contents included do not in any way supplement or replace legal advice obtained by a qualified and licensed attorney.

The information provided herein is based solely upon my professional experiences in the areas of New Jersey divorce and family law. While every effort has been made to ensure that the information contained in this book is helpful and of high quality, no representations or warranties of any kind are made with regard to the completeness or accuracy of the included content.

Please note that information provided within this guide is current as of publication date. Due to the complexity and frequency with which the divorce and family laws change, you should consult with a qualified attorney to determine the best course of action for your specific legal needs.

If you require legal advice based on the specifics of your case as it relates to New Jersey laws, please feel free to reach out to our office to schedule a consultation with one of our experienced attorneys. It would be our pleasure to help you.

For more information about other topics related to family law, such as divorce, alimony, domestic violence, prenuptial agreements, family mediation and child custody, domestic partnerships, or any other family law related topics, please ask us about our other books. All guides in the series are designed, like this one, to help you to make sound decisions regarding your family's individual situation. Please keep in mind, however, that these books contain general information, and not legal advice. Always direct specific questions about your own situation to an attorney.

Weinberger
Law Group, LLC
Family Lawyers: Safeguarding Your Future™

Letter from the Author

In addition to being a divorce and family law attorney, I am also the parent of a young child. The book you are now holding in your hands contains important information about how to file for or modify child support in New Jersey. However, before you dive in and begin to read all that we have put together for you, I would like to take a moment to speak with you parent-to-parent.

From my own life experiences, I personally understand the many reasons that may have led you to this moment of needing to address child support. I know that divorce, especially when children are involved, isn't easy, and this is likely a very difficult time for you and your family.

I also know -- and strongly believe -- that as a parent you want what is best for your children. In the process of calculating child support, it has been my experience that some people focus just on the final amount and lose sight of the fact that child support is meant to ensure that your children are able to lead healthy and productive lives, both now and in the future. In an extremely direct way, child support is at the heart of what parenting is all about: caring for your children by meeting their needs, no matter which parent they may be living with at the time.

When both parents embrace this notion of "putting children first," determining child support can turn into a surprisingly positive process for all involved. At the end of the day, doing right by your children is something that you will never regret.

Putting on my attorney hat, I want to encourage you to learn all you can about the many factors involved in calculating a New Jersey child support award. I created

this guide based on my years of experience working with families -- just like your own -- to create fair and reasonable child support related agreements. Trust me when I tell you that I have seen it all.

In the following pages, you will find commonplace examples, suggestions, and comprehensive child support information. My sincere hope is that after reading this guide, you will be better able to work out a child support award that best fits your child's needs and circumstances. However, you don't have to go through this process alone. We at Weinberger Law Group are here to empower you and your family by eliminating the confusion from the child support process. We will work with you to calculate the accurate support award and develop the proper strategy, placing your children's needs first and foremost.

If you are in need of legal assistance with your child support matter or any other divorce or family law matter, please do not hesitate to reach out to our firm for a free consultation. We are here to listen and offer you the legal support you need.

All my best,

Bari Z. Weinberger

Chapter 1

The ABCs of Child Support

If you are a parent going through separation or divorce, or if you have never been married to your child's other parent, you may wonder if you will have to pay child support or if you should seek child support payments. This e-book summarizes and explains the current New Jersey child support guidelines.

Understanding Child Support

Whether you are wondering if you have to pay child support, or whether you think you should receive it, either situation can be confusing and difficult. The good news is that New Jersey has one of the most well-defined sets of child support guidelines in the country. Although the rules can be complicated, it is worth taking the time to understand them if you find yourself on either end of a child support request.

How to Use this Guide

This book summarizes and explains the current New Jersey Child Support Guidelines. It is only a broad overview; the guidelines themselves are quite detailed, consisting of more than 100 pages of explanation, instructions, forms and charts. We link to relevant pages in the Guidelines as we discuss them. Please click on the link (or type in the web address) to see the section in the Guidelines as you read the description of how it is used and may be applied to your case.

Case studies located at the end of the book outline several common child support situations and arrangements. It may help to browse through these first to see where your situation might fit and then backtrack to the beginning of the guide to understand the legal steps leading to that particular child support award.

Please note that if you have a situation that is not specifically addressed either in this book or in the guidelines themselves, a New Jersey family law attorney will be able to provide information about how courts have interpreted the law in situations similar to your own.

> "New Jersey has one of the most well-defined sets of child suport guidelines in the country."
>
> Bari Z. Weinberger, Esq.

Chapter 2

Do I Need to Pay (Or Will I Receive) Child Support?

The most important piece of information contained in the Child Support Guidelines is the basic underlying assumption about child support in New Jersey, namely that children have the right to receive financial support from both of their parents.

Do I Need to Pay (Or Do I Have the Right To Receive) Child Support?

If this is a question that's foremost on your mind right now, consider Antonio and Jennifer's situation. The couple had been married for approximately nine years when they decided to divorce. At the time, their child was seven years old. Antonio worked as a store manager. Jennifer, after taking a few years off following their son's birth, was employed as a secretary in a large medical practice.

Since both had good jobs, and Antonio knew Jennifer would be able to get health insurance through her workplace to cover both herself and their son, Antonio went about filing for divorce with the belief that he would not be required to pay child support. After all, their son went to a public school and Antonio's mother could watch him after school for free until Jennifer was off from work. Plus, Antonio and Jennifer had discussed child custody and it looked like Antonio would take care of their son every weekend. That meant he would be paying for his son's food and care two days out of every seven, and his mom would be pitching in, so why the need for any support payments? Antonio skipped over all that information and thought Jennifer was doing the same.

Only Jennifer didn't skip this information and soon communicated with Antonio that she was seeking an order to establish temporary child support to cover their separation as well as a permanent child support order to be written into their divorce decree. At first, Antonio thought Jennifer's claim that he would need to pay court-ordered child support was simply an excuse to get revenge on him for leaving her. Then he consulted with an attorney who explained to him how child support in New Jersey works.

New Jersey Child Support Guidelines

In his conversation with the attorney, Antonio learned about the New Jersey Child Support Guidelines, a series of rules and calculation formulas that apply to child support actions brought in the state. The New Jersey court system has conducted extensive research and evaluation to ensure that the Guidelines treat parents as fairly as possible, taking into account virtually every conceivable parenting situation.

At its heart, the most important piece of information contained in the Child Support Guidelines is the basic underlying assumption about child support in New Jersey, namely that children have the right to receive financial support from both of their parents. In any situation where a child has parents who are not married to each other, the courts can therefore require both parents to contribute to the child's financial support. This applies to parents who were once married and are now divorced, or were never married.

States have different rules for determining how much support each parent should pay, and they base such rules on different economic principles. New Jersey courts follow the "Income Shares Model" of child support. Under this model, courts attempt to determine a total support amount that approximates the amount parents would spend on a child in an intact two-parent family, taking into account expenses such as childcare, medical insurance, and any factor the court deems best for the child. This amount is then split between the parents in proportion to their respective incomes.

"In New Jersey, children have the right to receive financial support from both parents."

Bari Z. Weinberger, Esq.

As Antonio's lawyer explained to him, this was why Antonio's mother offer to provide free childcare and his intention to cover 100 percent of weekend expenses -- while it may seem generous -- might not be enough to cover the amount of child support his son is entitled to receive. As initiated by Jennifer, the only way to know for sure how much child support needs to be paid is to apply the guidelines.

Establishing Child Support Amounts

What's next for Jennifer and Antonio? Generally speaking, if both parents can agree on an amount for child support based on the guidelines, a Consent Support Agreement will be established and no court appearance is necessary. If either parent does not agree on the amount of support, or there are other outstanding issues that must be settled, the parents will have to go to the Family Part of New Jersey Superior Court (often called Family Court), located in their county courthouse. The court will review the facts and issue an order. This order includes the amount to be paid and the way it will be paid.

Child support orders typically come in two forms:

Temporary: This form of child support is generally requested to cover child expenses when a couple is separated, but not yet divorced. There are two ways to achieve a temporary order for child support: reach an agreement yourselves concerning how to share expenses, or go to court and ask a judge to decide. In this latter situation, a court hearing to establish a temporary support order will be held.

Permanent: During divorce proceedings, a permanent child support order will be in place. The divorcing couple may arrive at an award through mediation, negotiation, or having a judge decide. Parents who were never married can achieve a permanent order through the same means. In some cases, a judge may first order paternity testing if the named party denies fathering the child, or other circumstances exist. More information on paternity testing is found at the Weinberger Law Group website: http://bit.ly/paternity-test.

Practical Tip: Familiarize Yourself with the Child Support Guidelines.

The current version of the New Jersey Child Support Guidelines is contained in Appendix IX to Court Rule 5:6A of the New Jersey Courts official website: http://bit.ly/csguidelines. You can read the guidelines on-line and/or print them out and keep them handy in a binder or folder. You can also obtain a copy from a family law attorney or from the law library at any New Jersey courthouse.

You will find that Appendix IX-A, located at the New Jersey Courts website: http://bit.ly/ix-a, contains an in-depth explanation of the philosophy, economic principles and general assumptions that underlie the guidelines. Appendix IX-B on the New Jersey Courts website: http://bit.ly/ix-b contains additional explanations, as well as line-by-line instructions for completing the guideline worksheets. In many cases parents may be able to avoid arguments over child support simply by familiarizing themselves with both Appendix IX-A and Appendix IX-B. If you don't understand all the legal language being used, it's still helpful to browse through to see the kinds of calculation worksheets you may eventually need to fill out. You can also ask your attorney to explain sections to you that seem unclear.

The full New Jersey Child Support Guidelines referenced throughout this book are located at the official New Jersey Courts website via these shortened URLS:

- Appendix IX-A: Considerations In The Use Of Child Support Guidelines, located at the official New Jersey Courts website: http://bit.ly/ix-a.

- Appendix IX-B: Use Of The Child Support Guidelines, located at the official New Jersey Courts website: http://bit.ly/ix-b.

- Appendix IX-C: Sole Parenting Worksheet, located at the New Jersey Courts official website: http://bit.ly/sole-worksheet.

- Appendix IX-D: Shared Parenting Worksheet, located at the official New Jersey Courts website: http://bit.ly/shared-worksheet.

- Appendix IX-F: Schedule of Child Support Awards, found at the New Jersey Courts official website, http://bit.ly/schedule-awards.

Chapter 3

Calculating Child Support

New Jersey's guideline child support amounts approximate the marginal (additional) cost to a family of raising one or more children. The amounts are based on studies that compared the expenses of economically similar families.

***Please note**: The full New Jersey Child Support Guidelines referenced throughout this chapter are located at the official New Jersey Courts website via the following URLS:*

- Appendix IX-A: Considerations In The Use Of Child Support Guidelines, located at the official New Jersey Courts website: http://bit.ly/ix-a.

- Appendix IX-B: Use Of The Child Support Guidelines, located at the official New Jersey Courts website: http://bit.ly/ix-b.

- Appendix IX-C: Sole Parenting Worksheet, located at the New Jersey Courts official website: http://bit.ly/sole-worksheet.

- Appendix IX-D: Shared Parenting Worksheet, located at the official New Jersey Courts website: http://bit.ly/shared-worksheet.

- Appendix IX-F:_Schedule of Child Support Awards, found at the New Jersey Courts official website, http://bit.ly/schedule-awards.

Calculating Child Support: General Principles

The specific steps involved in calculating child support are explained in more detail in the next section. The following is a brief overview of some of the most important principles of the guidelines:

- New Jersey's guideline child support amounts approximate the marginal (additional) cost to a family of raising one or more children. The amounts are based on studies that compared the expenses of economically similar families who either did or did not have children under the age of 18 living in the household.

- Courts understand that the guidelines are imperfect, but they consider them to be the best available estimates of the cost of raising children.

- Parents who have well-defined custody/parenting time arrangements can estimate the child support a court might order by consulting the guidelines and completing the applicable worksheets.

- Parents with less well-defined arrangements may need to work on a parenting plan before they can use the worksheets, as the appropriate application of the guidelines requires very specific information about how parents divide time with children. In constructing a parenting plan, it is important to keep in mind that determination of child support is not connected with legal custody of children, but only with the division of parenting time and with which parent pays actual direct costs of child support.

- New Jersey courts begin a child support calculation by using the basic formula set out in the Sole Parenting Worksheet Appendix (IX-C). In a shared parenting situation, where children's time with each parent exceeds approximately 28% of overnight time, a court has discretion to use the shared parenting formula set out in the Shared Parenting Worksheet (Appendix IX-D). Both formulas are explained in detail below.

- The Schedule of Child Support Awards (Appendix IX-F) sets out child support amounts that allocate the costs of raising a child to one household. These amounts include the child's share of total household expenses for housing, food, clothing, transportation, entertainment, unreimbursed health care up to and including $250 per child per year, and common miscellaneous items. To divide the costs appropriately between two households, parents must apply either the sole parenting or shared parenting formulas. These formulas make various adjustments for different categories of expenses ("variable," "fixed," and "controlled" expenses), as further discussed below.

> “Courts understand that the guidelines are imperfect, but they consider them to be the best available estimates of the cost of raising children.”

Bari Z. Weinberger, Esq.

- In both the sole parenting and shared parenting formulas, the first step in allocating responsibility for child support between parents is to determine each parent's net income. The next step is to find the appropriate child support amount for the parent's combined net incomes, and then assign each parent a percentage of that amount that matches the parent's percentage share of combined income.

- When children spend time in two separate households, it is appropriate to adjust child support to account for the percentage of time spent in each household. If a child is with one parent the majority of the time (approximately 72% or more of overnight time, as further defined by the guidelines) the adjustment will be calculated according to the Sole Parenting Worksheet (Appendix IX-C), and will apply only to "variable" costs, such as food, transportation, and occasional entertainment, typically born by a non-custodial parent during visitation, as these are generally the only costs of a custodial parent that would be reduced during the time the children are with a non-custodial parent.

- When parents share parenting time, and time with each parent exceeds approximately 28% of overnight time, it may be appropriate to allow an additional adjustment for "fixed" costs associated primarily with housing. This additional adjustment is addressed by use of the Shared Parenting Worksheet (Appendix IX-D). In the shared parenting formula, one parent is designated as the Primary Parent of Residence (PPR) and the other as the Parent of Alternate Residence (PAR). The PPR is either the parent with whom the child spends more overnight time or, if overnight time is equal, the parent with whom the child resides while attending school.

- The additional adjustment for fixed costs in the shared parenting formula allows the PAR a certain amount for housing costs, but it also results in an increase in the total amount of child support. In other words, the shared parenting formula acknowledges that both parents require housing that provides adequate day-to-day living space for children, rather than just enough space for children to spend the night occasionally, and that duplicating this type of housing results in greater overall costs.

- The guidelines assume that the PPR has static (unchanging) fixed expenses associated with maintaining housing for children at all times. Therefore, in the shared parenting formula, the PPR's fixed expenses are not reduced by the percentage of time a child spends with the PAR. The PAR will have an equal percentage of fixed expenses only when time-sharing is equal. This reflects the courts' priority of ensuring that a child has an adequate primary residence before allowing additional expenditures for an alternate residence.

- Due to the priority of first ensuring that children have an adequate primary residence, courts will not apply a shared parenting formula unless the parents meet certain minimum income requirements.

- The current guidelines assume that variable costs equal 37% of total childcare costs; fixed expenses equal 38% of total costs; and "controlled" expenses constitute 25% of total costs. Controlled expenses include items such as clothing, personal care products or services, most entertainment and most miscellaneous items. Regardless of whether the sole parenting or shared parenting formula is used, the guidelines assume that the custodial parent or PPR is responsible for virtually all controlled expenses. Such expenses are therefore not adjusted for parenting time, but only according to the parents' respective incomes. In an appropriate case, where, for example, parenting time is exactly equal and it is necessary to duplicate many controlled expenses, the parents could agree to an additional adjustment, or the PAR could request such an adjustment from the court.

- Additional expenses may be added to the child support amount. These include childcare expenses necessary to allow a parent to work, children's health insurance premiums, predictable and recurring unreimbursed health care expenses in excess of $250 per child per year, and other court-approved expenses. These expenses are further discussed below.

- Additional adjustments may be made under various circumstances. Income may be adjusted when a parent is not working but in the court's estimation could be working (or could be working more, or at a higher paying job). Support amounts may be adjusted when payment of the guideline amount would decrease the paying parent's income below a certain minimum amount; when a parent has other legal dependents; when there are multiple family obligations; when different children spend significantly different amounts of time with each parent; when a family member is receiving some type of government benefits; when children are teenagers at the time of an initial award; or when a child is over 18 and is no longer attending high school. These adjustments are further discussed below.

After making all applicable adjustments, the non-custodial parent or PAR will usually pay a percentage of the total award to the custodial parent or PPR. The PPR's or custodial parent's share is assumed to be expended directly on costs associated with child-rearing. In a shared parenting situation, depending on each parent's income and the amount of time children spend with each parent, either parent could end up paying support to the other.

Calculating Guideline Child Support

Either parent can estimate the amount of support a New Jersey judge would be likely to order by adding up both parents' combined total income and then completing either the Sole Parenting Worksheet (Appendix IX-C) or the Shared Parenting Worksheet (Appendix IX-D). Parents are required to file one of these worksheets with the court in any New Jersey Family Division case establishing or modifying support. As noted previously, the Use Of The Child Support Guidelines (Appendix IX-B) of the New Jersey Court Rules contains a detailed explanation of how income is determined for purposes of the guidelines (this is also summarized below), as well as line-by-line instructions for completing both the Sole Parenting and Shared Parenting Worksheets.

If you are a parent attempting to estimate support, you will use the same method to calculate net income and determine a basic support award regardless of which worksheet you choose. You can find the Basic Child Support Award by matching the total of both parents' net income to the appropriate column in the New Jersey Basic Child Support Award Schedule (Appendix IX-F). Both worksheets also allow additional expenses to be added to the basic support amount after making any applicable adjustments for fixed and variable costs. The major difference between the two worksheets is in the method of adjusting support amounts according to parenting time.

Choosing the Sole Parenting Worksheet:

In general, you should use the Sole Parenting Worksheet if one parent has physical custody of the children and the other parent is exercising visitation amounting to no more than 28% of parenting time. This is equivalent to approximately two regular overnight periods—or two periods of more than 12 hours each—per week, excluding vacation or holiday time. Consistent with the assumption that the parent a child lives with the majority of the time pays more direct costs of child-rearing and has higher expenses related to keeping an appropriate residence for the child (fixed expenses), the sole parenting calculation allocates more of the total net income available for support to the custodial parent and does not factor in an adjustment for the non-custodial parent's fixed expenses.

The Sole Parenting Worksheet does allow a deduction for the non-custodial parent's variable expenses, provided that such expenses reduce the variable expenses of the custodial parent. For example, if the non-custodial parent provides meals, drives the child places, and pays for occasional entertainment during visitation, this would typically result in lower food costs, gasoline costs and entertainment costs for the custodial parent, making a reduction in the child support amount appropriate. Nevertheless, if allowing the reduction in support results in the custodial parent having a total net household income (including the adjusted child support payment) of less than 200% of the poverty guideline for the number of persons in the household, the court can use discretion and decide not to allow the reduction. The priority is to first ensure a child adequate support in a primary household.

In addition to the deduction for variable expenses during regular visitation, a non-custodial parent can seek a partial abatement of support for variable expenses incurred during extended holiday or vacation visitation periods of five or more overnights. The final child support amounts are then adjusted for any supplemental expenses (as further discussed below), with each parent being responsible for these in proportion to their income.

Choosing the Shared Parenting Worksheet:

If your children are with each parent for the equivalent of more than two overnight periods per week (at least 28% of the time), you should begin with the Shared Parenting Worksheet. This worksheet designates one parent as the PPR and the other parent as the PAR. Parents using the Shared Parenting Worksheet must have a written parenting plan that has either been ordered by the court or agreed upon between the parents and filed in court. The plan must specify the division of parenting time and responsibilities between the parents with sufficient specificity for a court to determine whether or not use of the Shared Parenting Worksheet is appropriate. The PAR must not only demonstrate a sufficient amount of visitation time (the equivalent of at least two overnights a week), but must also show that separate living accommodations for the children will be maintained during overnight visitation.

After determining each parent's percentage share of income, the worksheet requires a calculation of each parent's percentage of parenting time based on the number of "overnights" the child spends with each parent. The PAR is then allocated an amount for fixed expenses, pro-rated based on the amount of time the child spends in the alternate household. This amount is calculated as two times the PAR's percentage of time with the child multiplied by the PPR's fixed expense amount. As noted above, the PPR's fixed expenses are not adjusted downward; the parents are allocated equal fixed expenses only when time-sharing is equal. The PAR's fixed expense allocation is added to the basic child support amount to determine the Shared Parenting Basic Child Support Amount.

Adding the PAR's time-adjusted fixed expenses to the basic support amount means that total support amounts are higher when two homes must provide overnight accommodations for children; the more time the child spends with the PAR, the higher the total costs. The PAR's time adjusted fixed expenses and percentage allocation of variable expenses are both subtracted from the PAR's share of the total support obligation. As with the Sole Parenting Worksheet, the numbers are then adjusted for additional expenses, with each parent being responsible for these in proportion to their income.

In some shared parenting situations a court will find use of the Sole Parenting Worksheet more appropriate. These include split parenting arrangements where there are multiple children and at least one child resides with each parent, and situations where the PPR's net household income from all sources would be less than twice the poverty guideline under the shared parenting calculation. Use of the Sole Parenting Worksheet in the latter type of situation reflects that in some cases the parents' combined income is simply too low to justify the additional expense required to establish a second residence for children and priority must be given to ensuring that they receive the basic necessities of life in their primary residence.

Calculating Income Available for Support

Gross and Net Income:

Guideline child support in New Jersey is based on the combined net income—gross income minus allowable deductions—of both parents. Gross income includes most types of earned or unearned income. Appendix IX-B contains a long list of sources of income that a court will ordinarily include as available gross income. The list is not exhaustive; courts may consider income not specifically included in the list. In considering whether or not to include a particular income source, a court will look at whether or not the income would normally be available for child-related expenses in an intact two-parent family unit. Common examples of gross income are wages, commissions, self-employment income, bonuses, dividend or interest income, alimony, rents received, worker's compensation or unemployment insurance benefits, and pensions.

Non-Taxable Income:

Non-taxable income such as worker's compensation benefits must be listed separately from taxable income, as a withholding allowance is calculated based on the taxable income only. The Use Of The Child Support Guidelines (Appendix IX-B) specifies four alternate methods of calculating withholding. You must identify which method you have used in the worksheet comments section.

Excluded Income:

A few types of income are excluded from gross income. These include means-tested (income based) public assistance benefits such as Temporary Assistance to Needy Families, Supplemental Security Income or the value of food stamps; mandatory nontaxable retirement contributions; child support a parent receives for children from another relationship; and the net amount of alimony or spousal maintenance a parent pays to a current or former spouse. If one parent will be paying alimony to the other in connection with a current divorce (with the exception of *pendente lite* alimony), the alimony amount should be determined first so that it can be included in the income of the receiving parent and excluded from the income of the paying parent. The Use Of The Child Support Guidelines (Appendix IX-B) contains some additional less common examples of income that may sometimes be excluded from gross income.

Government benefits that one parent receives specifically for support of children (such as income replacement benefits for disability or retirement, or other non means-tested benefits) are not included in income of the receiving parent, but the amount of the benefit will normally be deducted from the Basic Child Support Award. In a situation where the custodial parent or PPR is disabled and the deduction of the benefit from the PAR or non-custodial parent's support obligation would create a hardship in the child's primary household, the court may adjust or disallow the deduction.

Deductions from Gross Taxable Income:

Allowable deductions from gross taxable income include income taxes, mandatory union dues, and support that a parent pays for children of other relationships. If you have dependents from other relationship (legal or adopted children under age 18) that live with you, you may be able to deduct an amount for support of those dependents as well. You must ask the court to allow this deduction and you will have to provide the income of the other parent in the alternate family and complete a separate Sole Parenting Worksheet for that family. The adjustment requires three support calculations—a theoretical support amount for the dependents in the alternate family, a support amount that includes the other-dependent deduction, and a support amount that does not include the other-dependent deduction. Additional examples of possible deductions from gross income are listed in Appendix IX-B.

> **Practical Tip: Watch out for any potential effects of child support payments on benefits for special needs children.**
> Parents of special needs children need to be aware of the potential impact of child support payments on a child's eligibility for "means-tested" government benefits, such as Supplemental Security Income (SSI) and Medicaid. Although the benefits are not included in the parent's income for calculating support, receiving child support payments can affect the child's eligibility. It may be possible to minimize or eliminate this effect by structuring child support so that the non-custodial parent deposits payments into a trust set up for the child's benefit rather than providing payments directly to the custodial parent. You can contact a trust and estates attorney for more information about setting up a special needs trust.

Verifying Income:

Courts require parties to a child support hearing to submit either a Family Part Case Information Statement, found at the New Jersey Courts official website: http://bit.ly/family-cis (Court Rule 5:5-2), or a Financial Statement in Summary Support Actions, also found at the New Jersey Courts website: http://bit.ly/financial-statement (Court Rule 5:5-3) as verification of income. Courts determining gross income before June 30th of the current year will base findings primarily on federal and state income tax returns and supporting documents from the preceding year, such as W-2's and 1099's. Courts determining income after June 30th will use year-to-date income from all available documented sources, including paystubs, employer wage verifications, or statements of business receipts and expenses.

Assessing Self-Employment or Business Income:

If a parent is self-employed, derives income from participation in a business, or receives a similar type of income such as rent or royalty payments, gross income from the self-employment or business activity is calculated as gross receipts minus ordinary and necessary expenses of generating the receipts. Ordinary and necessary expenses do not normally include all of the expenses allowed by the IRS. In particular, home office expenses, business entertainment expenses, some types of depreciation expenses, and voluntary contributions to pension plans in excess of 7% of gross income are not allowable deductions for purposes of determining child support and must be included in available gross income. In some cases, gross income from a business may also include potential cash flow from sources such as loans taken from the business.

Assessing Fluctuating Income:

If a parent has sporadic or fluctuating income such as income from seasonal work, dividends, commissions, or bonuses, gross income will usually be determined by averaging the amount of the income over the previous 36 months, or from the time it was first received, whichever time period is shorter. Overtime or second job income will be averaged only for the most recent 12-month period. A parent who has sporadic income that is not expected to continue into the future can ask the court not to include it as income available for support.

Assessing the Value of Employment Benefits:

If a parent receives an allowance for housing or meals, such as a military allowance for quarters or subsistence, this is included in gross income. If the parent instead receives a significant employment benefit that reduces personal living expenses—such as subsidized housing, meals, or a company car—the value of such benefit should be included in gross income, regardless of the source of the benefit.

Imputing Income:

Parents cannot avoid their child support obligations by quitting a job or refusing to seek appropriate employment. A court that finds either parent is voluntarily unemployed or underemployed will estimate the parent's potential earning capacity in light of factors such as work history, training, education, and available jobs in the area, and may calculate child support based on such income. A court will sometimes base this "imputed" income on either a parent's former income or on the average earnings in the parent's former occupation as reported by the New Jersey Department of Labor. If no information about former income or occupation is available, a court may impute income based on hypothetical full-time employment (40 hours per week) at New Jersey minimum wage ($8.25 per hour as of January 2014).

In deciding whether or not to impute income to a parent, a court will consider what the probable employment status of a parent would have been had a two-parent family either formed or remained intact; the reasons for the unemployment or underemployment; the availability of alternate assets for support; and the presence of children in the household and child-care options. A parent caring for young children is entitled to an offset for any childcare expenses that would be necessary to work.

Adding Supplemental Expenses:

After calculating a basic support obligation according to the appropriate parenting worksheet, a court may add certain predictable and recurrent expenses to the award. These include the cost (after any applicable tax credits) of necessary work-related childcare, a parent's marginal cost of adding a child to a health insurance policy, and any predictable and recurring unreimbursed health care expenses exceeding $250 per child per year. These expenses are apportioned to the parents according to their respective incomes, and a parent who pays the expenses directly will receive a credit. Health care expenses that exceed $250 per child per year but are not predictable and recurring are not added to the child support order, but are shared by the parents in proportion to their relative incomes as they are incurred.

Guideline Deviations

Although the guidelines cover the vast majority of cases, there are many situations in which a court may order support that varies from the guideline recommendations. Courts have discretion to order a different amount in any situation where a deviation would be in the best interests of a child, provided that the child support order specifies in writing what the amount would have been had the guidelines been followed, and the reason for the deviation.

This law provides as follows:

In determining the amount to be paid by a parent for support of the child and the period during which the duty of support is owed, the court in those cases not governed by court rule shall consider, but not be limited to, the following factors:

- Needs of the child;
- Standard of living and economic circumstances of each parent;
- All sources of income and assets of each parent;
- Earning ability of each parent, including educational background, training, employment skills, work experience, custodial responsibility for children including the cost of providing childcare and the length of time and cost of each parent to obtain training or experience for appropriate employment;
- Need and capacity of the child for education, including higher education;
- Age and health of the child and each parent;
- Income, assets and earning ability of the child;

- Responsibility of the parents for the court-ordered support of others;
- Reasonable debts and liabilities of each child and parent; and
- Any other factors the court may deem relevant.

The obligation to pay support for a child who has not been emancipated by the court shall not terminate solely on the basis of the child's age if the child suffers from a severe mental or physical incapacity that causes the child to be financially dependent on a parent. The obligation to pay support for that child shall continue until the court finds that the child is relieved of the incapacity or is no longer financially dependent on the parent. However, in assessing the financial obligation of the parent, the court shall consider, in addition to the factors enumerated in this section, the child's eligibility for public benefits and services for people with disabilities and may make such orders, including an order involving the creation of a trust, as are necessary to promote the well-being of the child.

As used in this section "severe mental or physical incapacity" shall not include a child's abuse of, or addiction to, alcohol or controlled substances. (N.J.S.A. 2A: 34-23)

In addition to the statutory factors, the New Jersey Child Support Guidelines (Appendix IX-A) specify the following factors that courts may consider in making adjustments:

- equitable distribution of property in divorce,
- income tax consequences,
- fixed direct payments such as mortgage payments,

- a parent's unreimbursed medical or dental expenses,
- educational expenses for children,
- educational expenses required for a parent to improve earning capacity,
- the presence of more than six children in a single family household,
- special needs of gifted or disabled children,
- children's ages,
- any hidden costs of caring for children, including decreased income and career prospects, loss of saving, less time to shop economically,
- family units (i.e., one household) having more than six children,
- voluntary placement of children in foster care,
- a child's extraordinarily high income,
- pre-existing elder care obligations,
- tax consequences of health insurance payments, and
- multiple prior support obligations.

Some of these factors are discussed in more detail below. Parents must keep in mind that even this extensive list is not intended to be exclusive. Circumstances may exist both beyond those discussed in this book and beyond those discussed in Considerations In The Use Of Child Support Guidelines (Appendix IX-A). If you are wondering whether a deviation would be appropriate in your case, contact an attorney for advice.

Extraordinary Supplemental Expenses:

In some situations, a court will add predictable and recurring expenses beyond health care or child-care needed for work to a child support order. Depending on the circumstances of the particular case, such expenses may include private school tuition, expenses of special needs or gifted children, and transportation required for visitation. If your child has these types of expenses but one parent does not believe that they are necessary, the parent who is asking for the additional expense will have to present evidence of necessity to the court. The court will consider the expenses in light of the child's best interests and the ability of both parents to pay the expenses. Factors a judge will consider in deciding whether to include private school tuition, for example, would include the quality of available public schools in the area and the child's prior educational setting.

Any non-recurring special expenses agreed upon or ordered by the court will generally be shared by parents in proportion to their relative incomes. The custodial parent will usually be responsible for paying the expenses and for providing the non-custodial parent with receipts within a reasonable amount of time so that the non-custodial parent can provide reimbursement of a percentage share. If you anticipate your child having unpredictable special expenses, be sure that your agreement or court order specifically defines the type of expense that you and your child's other parent have agreed to split or that the court has ordered you to divide according to your respective incomes. A parent can object to providing reimbursement for any expense that falls outside the scope of the order or agreement.

Special Needs Children. Children with physical, mental, or emotional disabilities are more likely than other children to have both predictable and unpredictable health care expenses exceeding $250 per year, as well as various types of extraordinary supplemental expenses. Some examples of health care expenses that a court might add to a child support award include fees for speech, occupational, or physical therapy, home health care, psychological counseling, prescription medications, prosthetics, and assistive technology. If your special needs child has unusual expenses, their necessity will be evaluated the same way as any other extraordinary expenses, with the court considering both the child's best interests and both parents' combined ability to pay the expense. So, for example, if your spouse believes that the public school can provide your child with an adequate program by means of an Individualized Education Program (IEP), and you believe that only a full-time private school can meet your child's needs, you may have to provide expert testimony demonstrating both the need for the private program based on factors such as the child's precise condition and the demonstrated success of the private program as compared with the public alternative, and evidence supporting the ability of you and your spouse to pay for the program. A family law attorney who has a solid understanding of special education issues can be a valuable asset in this kind of situation.

Gifted Children. The guidelines specifically state that extraordinary expenses may also be justified for gifted children. A parent who wishes to claim such an expense will have to demonstrate that the child has a special gift or talent and that it is in the child's best interests to provide for the cost of nurturing the talent. This kind of extraordinary expense can cover a wide variety of goods and services, including special schooling, private tutoring, and assistive technology necessary to supplement the child's education.

Adjustments for Older Children:

The amounts specified in the guidelines represent the average cost of raising a child from birth through age 17. Studies show that expenses are higher than average for teen-age children and lower than average for preteen children. Where a child support order commences when children are young and continues through age 18, the amount will even out over time. However, if an award commences when children are in or near the teen years, a parent may request an adjustment to allow for the higher costs. The standard adjustment for orders entered when a child is 12 years of age or older is an increase of 14.6 % over the guideline amount. If the adjustment is part of the order, it should be noted in the worksheet or support order.

Payment of College Expenses:

New Jersey courts will sometimes order a parent to contribute to the support of a child over the age of 18 who is attending college full-time; however, courts must give priority to any minor children living in the home, and may not use the child support guidelines as a basis for awarding support for a college student over the age of 18 unless the student is living at home and commuting to college.

New Jersey case law has established a list of factors, called the "Newburgh factors," that a court should consider, in addition to any other relevant factors, in determining whether or not to require a parent to contribute to a child's college expenses. These factors are:

- whether the parent, if still living with the child, would have contributed toward the costs of the requested higher education,
- the effect of the background, values and goals of the parent on the reasonableness of the expectation of the child for higher education,
- the amount of the contribution sought by the child for the cost of higher education,
- the ability of the parent to pay that cost,

- the relationship of the requested contribution to the kind of school or course of study sought by the child,
- the financial resources of both parents,
- the commitment to and aptitude of the child for the requested higher education,
- the financial resources of the child, including assets owned individually or held in custodianship or trust,
- the ability of the child to earn income during the school year or on vacation,
- the availability of financial aid in the form of college grants and loans,
- the child's relationship to the paying parent, including mutual affection and shared goals as well as responsiveness to parental advice and guidance, and
- the relationship of the education requested to any prior training and to the overall long-range goals of the child.

Details of the Newburgh v. Arrigo, 88 N.J. 529, 545 (1982) case are available from the Google Scholar website: http://bit.ly/newburgh-v-arrigo.

If you are a parent seeking a contribution for a child's costs of attending college from the other parent, be sure to make a request for contribution before incurring actual expenses. A parent who is expected to contribute deserves to have the opportunity to be involved in the decision making process, and failure to seek such involvement can block later efforts to gain an order for contribution. Encourage your child to discuss plans with the other parent. Not only are efforts to involve the other parent likely to improve the chance of a successful legal claim for contribution, but parents who are asked to contribute will generally be much happier to do so if they feel that their opinions have been taken into account.

If you are the parent of a child who may want to attend college, it is a good idea to discuss plans with both your child's other parent and your child as the child progresses through high school. The ideal situation is to come up with a plan for financing your child's higher education that both parents and child agree on. If you have limited means, explore the possibility of public colleges and make sure that your child understands not only any limitations on your ability to contribute to financing but also any expectations you have regarding your child's grades, activities and potential contributions through part-time employment or scholarships.

“A court will apply the guidelines unless a party demonstrates that the circumstances of a specific case make application inappropriate or unfair.”

Bari Z. Weinberger, Esq.

Exceptions to the Guidelines

There is a "rebuttable presumption" that the New Jersey Child Support Guidelines govern payment of child support in any contested or uncontested action involving temporary or permanent child support. This means that a court will apply the guidelines unless a party demonstrates that the circumstances of a specific case make application inappropriate or unfair. In any such case, the court will consider factors set out in the New Jersey child support statute (NJSA 2A: 34-23).

A court that orders a non-guideline support amount after consideration of the statutory factors must state the reasons for deviating from the guidelines in writing. Parents who agree to a non-guideline support amount in a Marital Settlement Agreement also must state their reasons in writing. Common situations calling for deviation from the guidelines include extreme income situations:

Low Income. Courts recognize that parents who are unable to meet their own basic needs often lack incentive to work to pay child support. For this reason the guidelines contain safeguards to ensure that parents with extremely low income will not be left without any means of self-support. The guidelines call for application of a "self-support reserve, test" when one or both parents have income at or near the current U.S. poverty guideline. The "self-support reserve" is equal to 105% of the U.S. poverty guideline for one person ($224.42 per week as of January 17, 2014). If payment of child support according to the worksheet calculations would result in the paying parent having net income below the self-support reserve and the recipient parent having net income above the self-support reserve, a court is required to review the paying parent's income and living expenses carefully and determine the maximum amount of child support the parent could reasonably afford to pay. After considering all of the circumstances, the court will order support in an amount between $5.00 per week and the support amount designated in New Jersey Basic Child Support Award Schedule (Appendix IX-F) for parents with a combined net weekly income of $170 for the appropriate number of children.

High Income. In situations where parents have a combined annual net income—currently over $3,600 per week, or $187,200 per year—courts will begin by awarding the New Jersey Basic Child Support Award Schedule (Appendix IX-F) amount for the appropriate number of children based on a weekly income of $3,600, and will then add a discretionary amount based on the additional income after taking into account the factors (listed above) in the New Jersey Child Support Statute (N.J.S.A. 2A: 34-23). A court cannot simply extrapolate the New Jersey Basic Child Support Award Schedule (Appendix IX-F) support schedules out and add an amount proportional to the additional income, but must instead specifically consider the individual factors. The correct method of determining an appropriate additional support amount is to have the custodial parent or PPR prepare two separate budgets, one for the parent and child together and one for the parent alone. The parent's budget for the children should include two parts, one based on the parent's own income and the other including additional items that children need to be able to share in the economic status of the non-custodial parent or PAR. Examples of items for which a court might approve payment of additional child support include:

- private school tuition,
- private tutoring,
- summer camps,
- music or art lessons,
- sports clinics,
- vacations,
- study abroad,
- a car for a child of driving age,
- payments on a family car,
- costs of maintaining the child's primary residence,
- extra clothing and incidental items for teenagers,
- a 529 plan for college funding, and
- additional savings accounts or trusts on behalf of the children.

Not every set of parents with combined net income in excess of $187,200 will be expected to pay for all of the listed items; nor is the list exclusive. Courts recognize that high income may be fluctuating and that children's needs change over time. The basic principle underlying the analysis is that children are entitled to share in the standard of living of both of their parents and children of divorced parents should not lose the benefit of one parent's standard of living if they are no longer living with that parent. A parent's high income necessitates a careful calculation based on the needs of each individual child and the ability of each parent to pay for those needs.

Agreements between Parents:

Agreements parents make between themselves that provide for waiver of child support or for payment of some arbitrary amount of support are not valid, as the right to support belongs to the child rather than to either parent. However, if parents have agreed to an amount of child support which varies somewhat from the guidelines but still fulfills the needs of the children according to their best interests, a court will generally uphold the agreement. The agreement must include a child support guidelines worksheet showing what guideline support would have been in the absence of the agreement and must also state the reason for the deviation.

Obtaining a Copy of Your Child Support Order

Parents are entitled to know exactly how a court has calculated their child support award. Immediately following an initial award or any modification of an award, the court must provide each parent with a copy of the child support order. Parents may also request a copy of the guidelines worksheet used by the court, as well as any financial affidavits the court has relied on in determining the support amount.

Practical Tip: Be sure to account for all costs of childcare.

Making sure that you have accounted for all costs associated with raising children can be challenging. While the Case Information Statement (from the New Jersey Courts official website: http://bit.ly/case-statement) that you will file at the beginning of your case includes broad categories, such as "Sports and Hobbies," it can be easy to forget all of the costs a particular sport or hobby may include. Expenses that only come up occasionally are especially easy to miss. Make sure to include annual expenses in your monthly budget after dividing them by 12 to come up with a monthly figure.

Here are some examples of detailed cost breakdowns:

- ***Sports***—uniforms, equipment, team fees, photos, travel expenses

- ***Hobbies***—musical instruments or art supplies, dance or theatre costumes, lesson fees, photos, competition entry fees, club dues

- ***Education***—tuition, room and board, school books, tutoring, backpacks, yearbooks, field trips, teacher gifts, school photos, transportation, cost of a computer, computer supplies, applications and software, registration and admission fees, college test preparation fees, college application fees

- ***Entertainment***—movies, party gifts, costs of activities such as bowling or ice skating

- ***Transportation***—gas, parking, bus fare, ez pass, car washes, and any other costs of getting children to and from various activities

- ***Care of children's pets***—food, housing, bedding, toys, pet-sitting or boarding services, vaccinations and other veterinarian fees.

Chapter 4

Special Considerations in Military Child Support

If one or both parents are servicemembers in the United States military, certain options may be available when establishing child support. Depending on the branch of the military the parent serves under, slightly different rules may apply when calculating support or enforcing an existing child support order.

If you do not have an agreement or court order, and you are having difficulty obtaining support from a military spouse, you may be able to obtain assistance through the military command structure for the appropriate branch of service; however, obtaining relief in state court will generally provide you with superior protection as well as the ability to garnish wages for support. An attorney who practices military family law can provide additional information and will also be able to estimate the amount of support you might receive. The following is some very general information:

Branch Regulations:

The Air Force, Army, Marine Corps, and Navy all have slightly different regulations governing payment of child and spousal support in the absence of a court order or legal agreement between spouses. For example, the Navy uses equations requiring payment of different percentages of gross pay depending on whether there is a spouse only (one-third), a child only (one-sixth), a spouse and one child (one-half), and so on. The Army employs equations that vary depending on living arrangements and military or non-military status of the spouse, while the Air Force does not use equations at all and simply requires payment of adequate support, deferring to state courts for calculation.

“If you are having difficulty obtaining support from a military spouse, you may be able to obtain assistance through the military command structure.”

Bari Z. Weinberger, Esq.

Calculating Available Income:

Calculating income available for support from a servicemember's pay can be complicated. In New Jersey, benefits provided to the servicemember without cost in lieu of pay, such as a food or housing allowance, are included in the servicemember's gross income available for support. Accurate calculation of gross income requires imputing an appropriate amount for any such items, as well as examining the servicemember's LES to be sure that both basic pay and any special pay such as jump pay, dive pay, or flight pay is included.

Enforcing Support Payments:

A federal law known as the Servicemembers Civil Relief Act (SCRA) (50 App. USCA §§ 501-597B) protects active servicemembers from default judgments and allows a court to stay proceedings for a minimum of 90 days if current military service or service within the past 90 days is affecting a defendant's ability to appear and present a defense. Nevertheless, due to the urgency involved in ensuring temporary support for children and dependent spouses, in some cases it may be possible to obtain a court order for temporary child or spousal support even if the servicemember is attempting to stay the divorce proceedings. The servicemember may be able to participate in a temporary child support hearing by telephone conference. A competent attorney can provide assistance.

If necessary, spousal or child support wage garnishment can be effected through the Department of Finance and Accounting Service (the official DFAS site is found at: http://bit.ly/military-dfas). You will need an order from the court or from a child support enforcement agency

directing the government to pay the support amount and deduct it from the servicemember's earnings. Fortunately, default on a child or spousal support obligation by a military servicemember is a relatively uncommon occurrence, perhaps due to military guidelines which could justify a dishonorable discharge due to the default, or perhaps simply because of the high standards of honor and integrity generally attributable to individuals in the service.

Military families can visit the American Bar Association "HomeFront" website (official site found at: http://bit.ly/aba-military) to obtain additional information about applicable laws, including a more in-depth explanation of the SCRA.

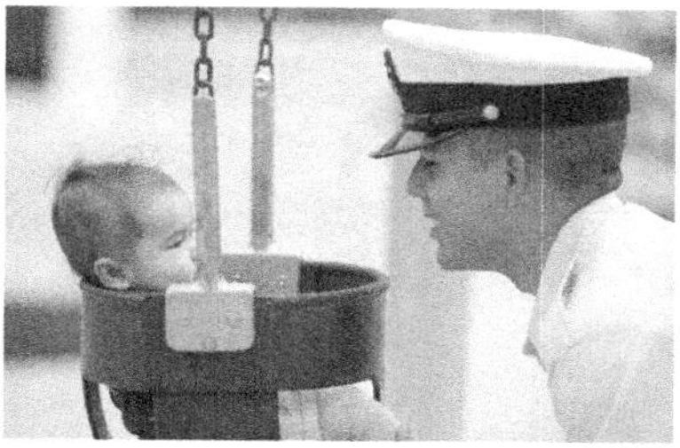

Chapter 5

Post-Judgment Matters Affecting Child Support

After a final child support order is put in place, issues can arise that require parties to return to court. Common post-judgment matters include the need for child support enforcement and requests to modify or terminate child support order based on changed circumstances.

For some parents, establishing an initial child support order puts an end to any need for court intervention. For others, circumstances arise that require additional procedures. There are two situations where this may occur:

- The parent obligated for the child support amounts stops paying, or

- A change of circumstances justifies a modification of the child support amount.

Motions to Enforce Litigant's Rights for Payment of Child Support

When one party fails to follow the terms of a court order, the other party's primary remedy will be to file a motion to enforce litigant's rights. This type of motion allows a party to ask the court to enforce previous orders and impose penalties on the party failing to comply, including, when appropriate, monetary sanctions. New Jersey Court Rule 5:3-7 (found at the official New Jersey Courts website: http://bit.ly/rule5-3) explains special remedies available following violation of orders regarding parenting time, alimony, or support.

In the child support context, a parent who is not receiving timely child support can file a motion to enforce litigant's rights. The motion can address regular support orders, as well as orders directing parents to maintain medical coverage for children, pay their designated share of unreimbursed medical related payments and all other financial obligations set forth in any written agreement or court order.

The superior court has the authority to order the responsible parent to bring all payments up to date, make future payments on time, and pay any attorney's fees the recipient has incurred in bringing the motion. The courts also have various tools available for ensuring compliance with orders for enforcement. A judge may be able to add part of an arrearage (past due support amount) to a regular wage-garnishment. If the non-paying party is unemployed but has substantial assets, the support recipient can ask the court to record the past due support amount as a judgment and direct the sheriff to seize assets such as bank accounts, or liquidate and sell other assets to satisfy the judgment. A recorded money judgment will also operate as a lien on any real estate the party owns.

In the most serious cases where a payer repeatedly disregards orders to bring payments up to date, a judge can issue a bench warrant for the party's arrest. This is a drastic remedy. Being in jail does not improve a party's ability to pay and may in fact make it considerably more difficult. Nevertheless, the threat of jail time does sometimes succeed in conveying the seriousness of the situation to a defaulting party when other methods have failed.

If you are the party responsible for paying child support, you must understand that this is a serious legal obligation. If you are having difficulty keeping up payments due to job loss or another personal hardship, you should consult an attorney about making a request for a modification. Failing to do this could result in any or all of the consequences outlined above.

If you need help in reorganizing your finances so that you can pay your support obligations and your other debts, you should consult with a credit counselor, a financial advisor, or an attorney to help you find options. Filing for bankruptcy may help you with other debts but it will not ameliorate your responsibility for paying support. Child support obligations take priority over many other types of debt and are not dischargeable in bankruptcy.

OCSS Options in Collection and Enforcement of Child Support Awards

The state agency responsible for helping parents obtain and enforce child support orders, including locating absent parents and establishing paternity, if necessary, is the Office of Child Support Services (OCSS) in the Division of Family Development of the New Jersey Department of Human Services (DHS). DHS records and monitors support due and paid through computerized records. The agency has several processes available to collect unpaid support and ensure that parents maintain medical insurance for children. The majority of the services offered by DHS are conducted through various county offices. OCSS works with the New Jersey Administrative Office of the Courts, county welfare agencies, county superior courts, and county probation divisions to provide comprehensive child support services. More information is available on the OCSS website. DHS maintains this interactive office locater tool (found at the official DHS website: http://bit.ly/office-locator) to help people identify which office can provide specific services. You can also contact OCSS by telephone at: 1 (877) NJ KIDS 1.

Parents can also get a basic idea of what amount of child support a court might order by accessing the quick calculator, available on the official DHS website: http://bit.ly/cs-calculator. This provides a very rough estimate only, however, and it is highly advisable to complete the appropriate worksheets and take into account all of the potential considerations discussed in this book and in the child support guidelines themselves rather than relying on the quick calculator.

“When a parent repeatedly disregards orders to bring child support payments up to date, a judge can issue a bench warrant for the party’s arrest.”

Bari Z. Weinberger, Esq.

Enforcement tools include:

1. **Income Withholding.** When a parent who has been ordered to pay child support receives a paycheck on a regular basis, income withholding (wage garnishment) is the preferred method of ensuring payment. The employer receives a notice of the court-ordered amount, including any applicable arrears (overdue amount), deducts it directly from the parent's paycheck, and then sends it to the New Jersey Family Support Payment Center. This center is commonly referred to as the Probation Department. The money is then distributed to the other parent. OCSS maintains a "New Hires Directory" to locate parents subject to child support orders and enforce payments. Employers in New Jersey are required to report new employees to the state within 20 days of hiring. If a parent is not receiving a regular paycheck but is receiving unemployment or worker's compensation benefits, the Child Support Program of the New Jersey Department of Labor can deduct support from these payments as well.

2. **Seizures and Offsets.** You can collect past due child support payments through several different methods. These include seizing assets such as bank accounts, stocks, bonds, funds awarded in a civil suit or settlement, or lottery winnings of $600 or more. A federal tax refund may be withheld and applied to unpaid support if the past due amount is at least $500, or $150 in a public assistance case.

New Jersey state tax refunds and homestead or saver rebates may be withheld to offset support payments that are one month or more in arrears.

3. **License Suspension.** When a parent has not paid court-ordered child support for at least six months, a court may order any licensing agency to suspend or revoke that parent's driving, professional, occupational, recreational or sporting license, or deny a parent's outstanding application for such a license. Any warrant for arrest based on non-payment of child support also includes an automatic suspension of the subject's driver's license.

4. **Passport Denial.** The U.S. State Department will deny an application for an initial or renewed passport to any parent who owes or has previously owed past-due child support of $2,500 or more. A parent can contest the denial by documenting that the arrears never exceeded $2,500, or that travel outside the country is necessary for employment, a serious medical emergency, or the imminent death of an immediate family member.

Other Remedies. Back support in excess of $1,000 can be reported to credit agencies. If a parent fails to appear for a court date to establish paternity, set a support amount, or enforce payment of support—or disregards a court order relating to child support—the family court may issue a warrant for the parent's arrest. A child support worker in the probation department can also file a motion to enforce litigants' rights on a parent's behalf.

Practical Tip: Keep accurate records of all payments and expenses.

Now more than ever, it is critical to keep track of your finances. Be sure that you document receipt or payment of any money that passes back and forth between you and your former spouse, including support payments, payments for expenses related to children, and any other incidental amounts. Note the amount of the payment, the date paid or received, the payment method and the purpose of the payment. Keep records of children's expenses that you believe the other parent should be paying for or contributing to, whether or not you are receiving such payment or contribution. Keep all of your documentation in a place that you will be able to locate easily in case you need to show it to your former spouse as a reminder or include it in an accounting for a future court date.

Modifying or Terminating Child Support

The court entering initial child support orders keeps jurisdiction until the children attain financial independence. This means that the court retains the power to make changes in child support payments whenever there is a substantial change in circumstances. In general, courts will not modify orders unless the change in circumstances has already occurred and is expected to continue indefinitely or for at least a considerable length of time.

If you have been paying child support for some time, or if you are receiving support and believe that your children need more, you may be wondering what you need to do to change the amount or end the payments. As with other post-judgment modifications, the initial burden of producing evidence that a change of circumstances has occurred is on the parent seeking the modification. Once a parent has provided initial evidence of circumstances justifying a change, the court will determine whether or not to hold a full hearing. The child support guidelines are subject to periodic administrative review and change, but a motion for an increase in support cannot be based only on the fact that there has been a change in the guidelines. There must be independent support for a change in the individual case.

The following are some common reasons people bring motions requesting a change in child support payments:

- an increase or decrease in either parent's income,
- a change in a child's needs,
- a change in parenting time,
- the birth of a new child,

- a child's emancipation (achievement of financial independence), or
- a child's enrollment in college.

Practical Tip: Do not put off addressing a change of circumstances situation.
While a court will not address a change of circumstances claim until after the circumstances have actually occurred, once the new circumstances are in place, it is important to bring a claim promptly (with some specific exceptions). People who wait months or even years before seeking a modification of support will generally find themselves shut out from the possibility of receiving retroactive relief.

Increase or Decrease in Income:

As with a request for a decrease in alimony payments, a request for a decrease or termination of child support payments must be based on a "good faith" (meaning not voluntary) decrease in ability to pay. An applicant will have to present documentation demonstrating a substantial and ongoing decrease in available income, including an updated Case Information Statement (CIS), recent tax returns, and W-2 statements or business records showing decreased income.

An applicant requesting a decrease in child support payments due to a job loss or pay-cut will need to provide documentation supporting efforts to become re-employed at the former level, or evidence supporting a claim that such re-employment is not possible, such as an updated resume and a log demonstrating efforts to find work. The loss of income must actually occur prior to the request for a modification, and the applicant will have to show that it is likely to continue on a long-term basis.

A parent can generally request an increase in child support for the same kinds of reasons that would justify a decrease. For example, a parent who has been laid off from a job can request an increase in the other parent's share of the support obligation if the lay-off is permanent and there is no comparable new position available. As with other requests for modification based on job loss or decreased income, the claim will require proof that the applicant is doing everything possible to become fully employed.

A parent whose income has decreased due to retirement will generally be able to obtain a decrease in child support payments as well; however, a court is unlikely to consider early retirement as a legitimate basis for reduction unless the parent has a very good reason for needing to retire and the modified child support will continue to be adequate for the child's needs. A request for modification based on a claim of disability must be based on sound medical testimony or evidence of an administrative determination of disability.

A request for a decrease in child support payments can also be based on a claim that the other parent's income has increased substantially, calling for a recalculation of the percentage share of support.

Change in a Child's Needs:

Children's needs often change over time. A child may develop trouble in school and require extra educational help, or demonstrate a special gift justifying lessons or attendance at enrichment programs or summer camp. Where the parents can both afford to pay for such things, a court might consider ordering the costs to be shared, even where one parent disagrees with the necessity.

Change in the Parenting Schedule:

A significant agreed upon change in the parenting schedule may call for a recalculation of support. A court will also recalculate support if one parent consistently fails to comply with the court-ordered schedule, and may also order that parent to pay the other parent's court costs and attorney's fees related to the recalculation.

Birth of Additional Children:

While remarriage alone does not trigger any change in child support payments, if one parent has additional natural or adopted children with a new partner after the court has set an initial support obligation, that parent can request that the child support obligation be recalculated to include the new child as a dependent. A court will not include stepchildren as dependents in the absence of some legal responsibility to support such children. A court that considers adjusting child support to allow for support of a new child will also consider the income of the new child's other parent and will impute income to that parent if appropriate. This type of recalculation would also be appropriate if for some reason a previously born child was not included in the original child support calculation.

A Child's Emancipation:

While New Jersey law does not fix a specific age at which a parent is no longer obligated to support a child, the child support guidelines are not applicable to children who are over 18 and have graduated from high school. When one child becomes "emancipated," meaning capable of self-support, a parent paying support can bring a motion requesting termination of support for that child. If the court agrees to terminate support, it will recalculate the child support award for any remaining unemancipated children based on the number of such children and the current income of both parents. If a child is not yet financially independent but has graduated from high school and is over 18, a parent can request an adjustment in the support amount based on consideration of all factors set forth in the New Jersey child support statute (N.J.S.A. 2A: 34-23).

A Child's Enrollment in College:

In some cases a New Jersey court will order a parent to contribute to a child's college or other post-secondary school expenses. When support orders are fixed while children are young, this contingency has rarely been taken into account, and if the parents cannot reach agreement on how to handle such expenses, a judge will intervene. The court will not order a continuation of support based on the child support guidelines, but will instead consider what kind of support might be appropriate based on the individual circumstances of the case.

FAQ: When does emancipation occur in New Jersey?

New Jersey law differs from laws in many other states in that there is no automatic age at which children reach emancipation. Although the child support guidelines do not apply to children over the age of 18, such children are often still entitled to child support. In New Jersey, emancipation occurs when a child goes "beyond the sphere of influence" which generally means that the child has turned 18 and obtained full-time employment. Courts generally consider children over 18 who are not employed full-time but are enrolled in post high school education, particularly full-time four-year colleges, to be still within the sphere of parental influence. For this reason, New Jersey courts often order divorced parents to share the cost of a child's college education based upon their respective abilities to pay, including imputed ability to pay in the case of an unemployed or underemployed parent. This is very different from the law in the majority of states, but serves to continue to aid children who remain dependent.

Child Support Case Studies

Child Support Case Studies:

1. Example of a Child Support Calculation using the Sole Parenting Worksheet
2. Example of a Child Support Calculation using the Shared Parenting Worksheet
3. Resolution of Child Custody and Child Support between Never-Married Parents
4. Resolution of Child Custody and Child Support without Court Appearance by Father
5. Payment of College Educational Expenses as Child Support
6. Child Support Enforcement Granted with Measures to Collect Past-Due Support
7. Motion to Enforce Child Support through Property Lien Granted where Parent Unavailable
8. Child Support Modification Granted after Birth of New Child
9. Modification of Alimony and Child Support Denied Due to Voluntary Nature of Unemployment

Please note: *the following case studies contain fictional and non-fictional scenarios. All of the parties' names have been changed to protect the privacy of the families.*

1. Example of a Child Support Calculation using the Sole Parenting Worksheet

Sarah and John Dexter are separating after an eight-year marriage. They have two children, Elijah, 4 and Jessica, 6. John works long hours managing a business. He currently earns a salary of $75,000 per year. Sarah has been a stay-at-home parent since Elijah's birth four years ago, but prior to this she worked as a dental hygienist for several years.

Sarah and John attended private mediation to work out their disputes regarding alimony, child custody, and child support. They agreed quickly that due to John's schedule a fairly traditional custody and visitation plan made the most sense. They initially agreed that the children would live primarily with Sarah and spend alternate weekends and one evening per week with John. John wanted more time than this and was especially concerned with staying involved in the children's weekend activities. Jessica had recently joined a soccer league that practiced every Saturday, and John was currently coaching her team. After some discussion, John and Sarah agreed that instead of one evening per week, it made more sense for John to plan a separate weekly activity with each child and keep the time flexible, so that he could sometimes schedule it on the weekends when the children were spending most of the weekend with Sarah.

A bigger source of disagreement was Sarah's continuing status as a stay-at-home parent. John insisted that she try to find some work, arguing that now that they had two households to maintain, there was no way that his paycheck could continue to support all of them. Sarah agreed to investigate work opportunities. She eventually found a part-time job that would allow her to work 20 hours per week while the children were in school. She would earn approximately $600 per week. John agreed that it made sense for the time being for her to limit her schedule to part-time, but insisted that she consider adding more hours going forward. Sarah argued that both the nature of her career and the fact that the children were very young made it difficult to guarantee that she would be able to find full-time work at any particular time. John stated that since they had been married only eight years, he was not willing to pay her alimony for any longer than four years when she was capable of supporting herself. At the end of their negotiations, they agreed that John would pay Sarah $300 per week in alimony for four years and that they would base the child support calculations on the assumption that she would have income of $900. They agreed that by the end of the four-year period, Sarah should be able to earn at least that additional $300 per week on her own.

John and Sarah now had a reasonable set of numbers on which to base a child support calculation. (Please note that several of these numbers have been simplified for the purpose of completing this example.) Following along with the appropriate line items on the Sole Parenting Worksheet (found at the official New Jersey Courts website: http://bit.ly/sole-worksheet) their calculations look like this:

- L.1-3: Non-custodial parent (John) adjusted weekly gross taxable income: ($1442 in wages - $300 alimony = $1142) - $420 tax withholding* = Net Taxable Income of $722.

- L.1-3: Custodial parent (Sarah) adjusted weekly gross taxable income: ($600 in wages + $300 alimony = $900) - $175 tax withholding* = Net Taxable Income of $725.

- L.6: Total Net Income for both parents: $1447.

- L.7: Each parent has approximately 50% of the available income.

- L.8: The Basic Child Support Amount for two children (From Appendix IX-F Schedules) is $319.

** If you are calculating income that is partly alimony and partly earned income, be aware that there may be a difference in tax withholding between the two types of income. For this example, we have used simplified and somewhat arbitrary tax withholding numbers to avoid over-complicating the scenario. See Appendix IX-A (http://bit.ly/ix-a) and Appendix IX-B (http://bit.ly/ix-b) for a complete explanation of the withholding rules.*

2. Example of a Child Support Calculation using the Shared Parenting Worksheet

Lisa Brogan and Paul Granville recently decided to separate after being married for 10 years. They have two children together, Anna, age 10, and Elisa, age 7. Paul is a systems analyst and earns approximately $110,000 per year. Lisa is the director of a day care center and earns $55,000 per year. Both Paul and Lisa wanted primary custody of the children, but after a brief period of negotiation, they agreed that a parenting plan that matches their current parenting responsibilities as closely possible would give them nearly equal time and make the most sense.

Lisa works from 7 a.m. to 3 p.m., which permits her to be home at about the same time the children get out of school each day. Paul typically works until 5 or 6 p.m., but he is able to telecommute up to two days per week, which has allowed him to be home often during school holidays or if one of the children was ill. Lisa and Paul decide to try a modified split week schedule. Paul will telecommute on Thursdays and Fridays. He will pick the children up from Lisa's apartment at 5 pm on Wednesdays and Lisa will pick them up from Paul's apartment at 5 pm on Saturdays. Because this splits the weekends, they agree that they will maintain flexibility and adjust the schedule to allow each of them a full weekend once every month or two. They also agree to share equal time on school holidays, and that each of them will have a two-week period with the children each summer so that they can take a vacation together. They work this out on a calendar, which shows that Lisa will have 190 overnights with the children and Paul will have 175.

They agree to use the Shared Parenting Worksheet (found at the official New Jersey Courts website: http://bit.ly/shared-worksheet) with the following calculations:

- L.1-3: Parent of Primary Residence (PPR/Lisa) weekly gross taxable income of $1058 in wages - $230 tax withholding (simplified) = Net Taxable Income of $828.

- L.1-3: Parent of Alternate Residence (PAR/Paul) weekly gross taxable income of $2115 in wages - $700 tax withholding (simplified) = Net Taxable Income of $1415.

- L.6: Total Net Income for both parents: $2243.

- L.7: Paul has approximately 63% of the available income and Lisa has approximately 37%.

- L.8: The Basic Child Support Amount for two children (From Appendix IX-F Schedules) is $396.

- L.9: Lisa has 190 overnights and Paul has 175.

- L.10: Lisa's percentage share of overnights is 52% and Paul's is 48%.

- L.11: The PAR Shared Parenting Fixed Expenses are equal to the basic support amount ($396) x Paul's percentage share of overnights (48%) x 38%, x 2, or $144.

- L.12: The Shared Parenting Basic Support Amount is increased by $144, to $540.

- L.13: Paul's share of the shared parenting basic support amount is 63% of $540, or $340. Lisa's share is 37%, or $200.

- L.14: The PAR share of variable expenses is Paul's percentage of overnights (48%) x the basic child support amount of $396 time x .37, or $70.

- L.15: The PAR adjusted Shared Parenting Basic Child Support Amount is Paul's share ($340) – the Par share of fixed expenses ($144) – the PAR share of variable expenses ($70), or $126.

- L.16: The parties do not need childcare.

- L.17: The children currently have health coverage through Lisa's employment at no additional cost to her.

There are no additional adjustments. Paul will pay Lisa $126 dollars per week to cover his share of expenses for the children while they are in her care. As the PPR, Lisa is assumed to pay her share of child-care expenses directly.

3. Resolution of Child Custody and Child Support between Never-Married Parents

The following case illustrates the legal obligation of a parent to support a child financially, regardless of the parent's level of involvement in the child's life. It also serves as a warning against trying to ignore or wish away the consequences of pregnancy out of wedlock. Denial could, in fact, simply exacerbate the issues:

Stacey and Peter have never been married. They have one child together, a little girl named Belinda, who is currently four years old. When Peter and Stacey were dating, Peter knew he was not ready to be a parent, but he and Stacey failed to take sufficient precautions against possible pregnancy. When Peter learned that Stacey was indeed pregnant, he declared that he did not wish to be a part of the baby's life. He broke off his relationship with Stacey and requested that she sever all contact with him.

In spite of Peter's expressed wishes, Stacey notified him when Belinda was born. Much to Stacey's disappointment, Peter repeated that he did not wish to be involved with the child in any way. Since Belinda's birth, Stacey has been her exclusive caretaker. Although Stacey continued to extend invitations to Peter encouraging him to become involved in Belinda's life, he steadfastly stood by his decision to remain out of the picture, either restating his wishes each time Stacey contacted him, or ignoring her communications entirely. It was difficult for Stacey to support Belinda financially by herself and she frequently asked Peter to make a contribution, but he ignored these requests as well.

As Belinda approached kindergarten age, Stacey realized that she needed to formalize legal custody to be sure that she would be able to make all parenting decisions on her own. She filed papers in court requesting sole physical and legal custody. In the same proceeding, she asked the court to compel Peter to pay child support and to implement wage garnishment to make sure that he complied.

Peter had full notice of the court proceedings. He filed a response stating that he had no involvement in Belinda's life and no wish to be involved, and that therefore he did not believe he should be obligated to pay child support. On the return date, he appeared in court and repeated this position to the judge. The judge awarded sole legal and physical custody of the child to Stacey.

Was Peter off the hook financially? Not at all; the judge ordered him make child support payments in the amount fixed by the New Jersey Child Support Guidelines. Peter's child support payments are currently being garnished from his paycheck by the county probation department.

4. Resolution of Child Custody and Child Support without Court Appearance by Father

The following case is similar to the previous one, but also illustrates how a court can order a parent to pay child support even if the parent does not participate in court proceedings:

Kim was eight and a half months pregnant with her baby girl when she retained counsel. Kim and Martin had been in a dating relationship for several years but never married. When Martin learned of Kim's pregnancy, he ended their relationship and broke off contact with Kim. Martin made it very clear at that time that he did not want the child and had no intention of helping Kim with child support.

Commensurate with the birth of the child, Kim's attorney filed a complaint asking the court to award sole legal and physical custody of the baby to Kim, along with a motion asking the court to order Martin to pay for hospital related costs and expenses as well as child support via wage garnishment. Kim's attorney notified Martin of the proceedings but he chose not to participate. He provided no information regarding employment or income. Nevertheless, the court held that Martin was responsible for paying medical costs related to the child's birth plus child support to Kim on behalf of their daughter. The court awarded Kim sole legal and physical custody and calculated child support by utilizing the New Jersey Child Support Guidelines – Sole Parenting Worksheet, imputing income to Martin in the amount designated on his prior year's tax return and W-2 forms.

5. Payment of College Educational Expenses as Child Support

This case demonstrates how a New Jersey court might allocate payment of college expenses between divorced parents. This case required a post-judgment motion to modify child support payments:

Jeremy and Lynn were divorced five years ago after a 15-year marriage. They executed a settlement agreement at the time of their divorce but deferred the issue of college contributions for their child, Kyle, as he had not yet started high school. They felt that the decision should be based on the actual financial circumstances of each parent as Kyle approached college age. At the time of the divorce, Jeremy and Lynn had a 529 Education Account for Kyle with a balance of about $20,000.

During Kyle's junior year in high school Jeremy earned $150,000 plus an additional $20,000 in annual bonus pay. Lynn was currently earning $60,000 per year. Kyle was admitted to both Rutgers University and New York University. He had a GPA of 3.9. His transcript included a considerable number of Advanced Placement classes.

Kyle wished to attend NYU so that he could take advantage of a special program that fit his future goals more closely than the program offered at Rutgers. He had demonstrated a dedication to this particular area of study throughout high school and had performed volunteer work in the area for the past 3 years. Kyle had received a scholarship from NYU consisting of a $2,500 per year contribution toward annual tuition, for a total of $10,000. He had also received a scholarship from Rutgers in the amount of $8,000 total over four years.

Jeremy was willing to contribute a percentage share of Kyle's total tuition based on his higher income, but he argued that the contribution should be capped at the amount of the Rutgers University tuition, rather than the substantially higher tuition charged by NYU. Lynn's position was that Kyle should be able to attend NYU because of the dedication he had shown and the combined ability of his parents to contribute to the costs of school. She argued that each parent's contribution should be based on the total costs of attending NYU, including not only tuition, but also room, board, and other educational expenses.

The court ordered Kyle's parents to contribute to his costs of attending NYU. Kyle would be required to apply all available 529 and other education accounts, scholarships, loans, grants and all other forms of financial aid, before either parent's obligation would come into play. After deducting funds from these sources, Jeremy would be responsible for paying 75% of the remaining educational expenses and Lynn would be responsible for paying 25%. Educational expenses were to include admission fees, tuition, room, board, books, lab/computer and other institutional fees, and reasonable costs of transportation to and from school. The court also ordered Jeremy to reimburse Lynn for 75% of all application fees and standardized test preparation course fees that she had paid for Jeremy.

6. Child Support Enforcement Granted with Measures to Collect Past-Due Support

This case shows how a court might handle collection of a large amount of past due child support:

Carmen and Mark were divorced four years ago. Their only child, Kevin, is currently ten years old. Based on the income available to each parent at the time of the divorce, the court ordered Mark to pay $180 per week in child support directly to Carmen. In spite of repeated requests from Carmen, however, Mark consistently failed to make the payments. The amount of back support he owed gradually climbed to a total of $29,800.

Carmen repeatedly asked Mark to become current with the payments but he continued to ignore her requests. She applied to the court for enforcement of the child support order, asking the court to find Mark in violation of his payment responsibility and order him to begin making timely and complete payments, as well as begin bringing the accrued arrearage (past-due amount) up to date.

The court granted Carmen's application, holding Mark in violation of the child support order and placing him on a two-week bench warrant status. This action by the court meant that unless Mark made complete payments on time and in full for two consecutive weeks, he could be arrested and incarcerated, with his release from jail conditional upon satisfaction of the payments.

In addition, the court also ordered Mark to make a good faith down payment toward his existing arrearage in the lump sum of $5,000 within 14 days of the order, with another $2,500 due within the following 60 days. Mark's anticipated tax refund in the amount of approximately $4,000 was also garnished to help satisfy the arrearage, and the court ordered him to liquidate a modest retirement account to further pay down the amount.

To accommodate pay-down of the arrearage that would still be outstanding after these payments were applied, the court increased Mark's weekly child support payments from $180 per week to $250 per week. Going forward, payments would be made through the appropriate probation department by means of wage garnishment.

7. Motion to Enforce Child Support through Property Lien Granted where Parent Unavailable

When a parent responsible for paying child support is living out of the country and chooses to avoid the support obligation, gaining access to funds for support can be challenging. This case illustrates how property in the state can be used to satisfy the obligation even if the parent is not available:

Alicia and Peter were married for ten years and had two children together, Jake and Carrie. At the time of their divorce, the court ordered Peter to pay child support to Alicia on behalf of Jake and Carrie. Peter complied with the obligation for a few years and then suddenly stopped paying. He also stopped visiting the children. He did not inform Alicia of the reasons for his stark change in behavior, and she was not able to contact him for several months.

Eventually Alicia learned that Peter had moved to Colombia to work with his brother. She was unable to obtain a specific new address. Peter was remarried and his new wife continued to live in New Jersey in a house that Peter owned. He also owned another small apartment located adjacent to the New Jersey property. This apartment was currently rented to two tenants. Alicia's attorney filed a motion to enforce Peter's child support obligation, asking the court to garnish the rental income in satisfaction of the child support arrearage as well as Peter's share of unreimbursed medical expenses for the children.

The court found that the property located within New Jersey was the only source of income currently accessible for satisfaction of the support obligation. The court could not realistically force Peter to appear in court; even an arrest warrant would be essentially useless unless he chose to return to New Jersey voluntarily. The court placed a lien on the rental property on Alicia's behalf, so that she could collect the rental income in satisfaction of Peter's child support obligation and the unreimbursed medical expenses.

8. Child Support Modification Granted after Birth of New Child

Ryan and Haley were divorced five years ago. At the time they had two children, Chelsea, age six and Alan, age eight. They entered into a settlement agreement requiring Ryan to pay child support to Haley in the amount of $360 per week.

Ryan has since remarried and his new wife has just given birth to Ryan's third child. Ryan applied to the court requesting a downward modification of his child support payment for the two children from his first marriage based on the "Other Dependent Deduction," which permits a parent to recalculate child support to add an additional legally dependent child. He supplied the court with supporting documents, including the original settlement agreement, his Case Information Statement from the original divorce case, an updated Case Information Statement, proof of current income, proof of his new wife's income, and completed child support guideline worksheets.

The court granted Ryan's application and lowered the payments he was required to make to Haley for support of their children, based on the fact that his income now needed to stretch to accommodate support of an additional child.

9. Modification of Alimony and Child Support Denied Due to Voluntary Nature of Unemployment

This case demonstrates that unemployment is not a change in circumstances that will justify a modification of a support obligation if the unemployment is essentially voluntary:

Jennifer and Jason had been married for 24 years and had three children together. Jason was the primary breadwinner throughout the marriage and at the time of the divorce, Jennifer had not worked in almost 20 years. The court ordered Jason to pay child support and permanent alimony to Jennifer.

Approximately one year after the divorce, Jason filed a motion for modification of his support obligations based on the fact that he had decided to accept a severance package from his employer and was no longer working. Jason claimed that he had made this decision on the basis that he suffered from a form of arthritis that prevented him from continuing in his current job. Jennifer's attorney filed an opposition to Jason's motion arguing that he had not provided any medical documentation of his alleged disability and had not applied for Social Security disability benefits. He also had not demonstrated that he was unable to continue any kind of gainful employment and had failed to provide documentation showing a good faith attempt to obtain another job.

The court found that Jason's unemployment was voluntarily and that he was therefore unable to establish the substantial change in circumstances required for a modification of his support obligations. The court denied his motion and ordered him to continue paying alimony and child support in the original amounts.

Further Information and Resources:

- Weinberger Law Group provides up-to-date information about child support law in New Jersey on its child support pages, located at: http://bit.ly/support-guidelines.

- For additional information about emancipation of a child in the state of New Jersey, see "New Jersey Emancipation of a Child," on the Weinberger Law Group website: http://bit.ly/child-emancipation.

- For additional information on how courts take payment of private school or college tuition into consideration when calculating child support, see "New Jersey Educational Expenses in Child Support Calculations," on the Weinberger Law Group website: http://bit.ly/educational-expenses.

- The law governing New Jersey child support in cases not covered by the Court Rules and Appendix IX is contained in N.J.S.A. 2A: 34-23. This statute lists the factors set out in this book under *Extreme Income Situations:* High Income. The full text of N.J.S.A. 2A: 34-23 is available on-line at the New Jersey Legislatures website: http://bit.ly/nj-leg.

- You can find additional information about paying, receiving, and enforcing child support on the Office of Child Support Services (OCSS) website: http://bit.ly/nj-child-support.

The full New Jersey Child Support Guidelines referenced throughout this book are located at the official New Jersey Courts website via these shortened URLS:

- Appendix IX-A: Considerations In The Use Of Child Support Guidelines, located at the official New Jersey Courts website: http://bit.ly/ix-a.

- Appendix IX-B: Use Of The Child Support Guidelines, located at the official New Jersey Courts website: http://bit.ly/ix-b.

- Appendix IX-C: Sole Parenting Worksheet, located at the New Jersey Courts official website: http://bit.ly/sole-worksheet.

- Appendix IX-D: Shared Parenting Worksheet, located at the official New Jersey Courts website: http://bit.ly/shared-worksheet.

- Appendix IX-F: Schedule of Child Support Awards, found at the New Jersey Courts official website, http://bit.ly/schedule-awards.

Family Law Departments

Atlantic County
Atlantic County Civil Courthouse
Family Division, Direct Filing
1201 Bacharach Blvd., West Wing
Atlantic City, NJ 08401
(609)-345-6700

Bergen County
Justice Center, Room 119
10 Main Street
Hackensack, NJ 07601
(201)-527-2300

Burlington County
Burlington County Central Processing Office
Attention: Dissolution Intake
Courts Facility,
1st Floor, 49 Rancocas Road
Mount Holly, NJ 08060
(609)-518-2645

Camden County
Camden County Family Division
Hall of Justice
2nd Floor, 101 S. 5th Street
Camden, NJ 08103-4001
(856)-379-2204

Cape May County
Superior Court Chancery, Family Part
4 Moore Road
Cape May Courthouse, NJ 08210
(609)-463-6600

Cumberland County
Cumberland County Family Division
60 W. Broad St.
Bridgeton, NJ 08302
(856)-453-4564

Essex County
Family Division Dissolution Unit
Wilentz Justice Complex, Room 113
212 Washington Street
Newark, NJ 07102
(973)-693-6710

Family Division Non-Dissolution Unit
Wilentz Justice Complex, Room 1365
212 Washington Street
Newark, NJ 07012
(973)-693-5560

Gloucester County
Family Division
Gloucester County Justice Complex
70 Hunter Street
Woodbury, NJ 08096
(856)-686-7400

Hudson County
Family Intake Team Administration Bldg., Room 203
595 Newark Avenue
Jersey City, NJ 07306
(201)-795-6777

Hunterdon County
Family Case Management Office
Hunterdon County Justice Center
65 Park Avenue
Flemington, NJ 08822
(908)-237-5920

Mercer County
Family Case Management Office
175 S. Broad St., 2nd Floor
P.O. Box 8068
Trenton, NJ 08650-0068
(609)-571-4200

Middlesex County
Family Part Intake Reception Team
Family Courthouse
120 New St., Room 111
P.O. Box 2691
New Brunswick, NJ 08903-2691
(732)-519-3242

Monmouth County
Family Part, Courthouse
71 Monument Park
P.O. Box 1252
Freehold, NJ 07728-1252
(732)-677-4050

Morris County
Morris County Family Division
Morris County Courthouse Family Intake
Washington and Court Streets
P.O. Box 910
Morristown, NJ 07963
(973)-656-4000

Ocean County
Ocean County Justice Complex
Family Practice Division
120 Hooper Avenue, Room 210
Toms River, NJ 08754
(732)-929-2033

Passaic County
Passaic County Superior Court Family Part
County Administration Bldg. 8th Floor
401 Grand Street
Paterson, NJ 07505
(973)-247-8459

Salem County
Family Court Intake
Courthouse
92 Market St.
Salem
NJ 08079
(856)-878-5050 x.15771

Somerset County
Family Case Management Office
Courthouse, 2nd Floor
P.O. Box 3000
Somerville, NJ 08876-1262
(908)-231-7600

Sussex County
Sussex County Family Division
Sussex County Judicial Center
43-47 High Street
Newton, NJ 07860
(973)-579-0630

Union County
Dissolution Assignment Office
New Annex Bldg; Courthouse
2 Broad Street
Elizabeth, NJ 07207
(908)-659-3314

Warren County
Family Division Dissolution Unit
Courthouse
413 Second St.
P.O. Box 900
Belvidere, NJ 07823-1500
(908)-475-6150

For More Information

At Weinberger Law Group all of our attorneys are engaged full time in the practice of family law. We are committed to providing honest recommendations and keeping the best interests of our clients and their children at the forefront at all times. Our attorneys will strive to resolve your matter out of court and will explore your settlement options, including New Jersey divorce mediation if appropriate in your case. When necessary, we will also fight vigorously to protect your rights.

You can find out more about our dedicated family law attorneys on our website, which is located at: www.weinbergerlawgroup.com. Weinberger Law Group offers an initial consultation with an experienced New Jersey Family Law Attorney at no cost.

Weinberger Law Group has several offices located throughout New Jersey.

Weinberger Law Group Headquarter Offices:
119 Cherry Hill Road, Suite 120
Parsippany, NJ 07054
Morris County

Tel: (888) 888-0919

Weinberger
Law Group, LLC
Family Lawyers: Safeguarding Your Future™

Other Titles In The Weinberger Law Group Library Series

Available now:

Coming soon:

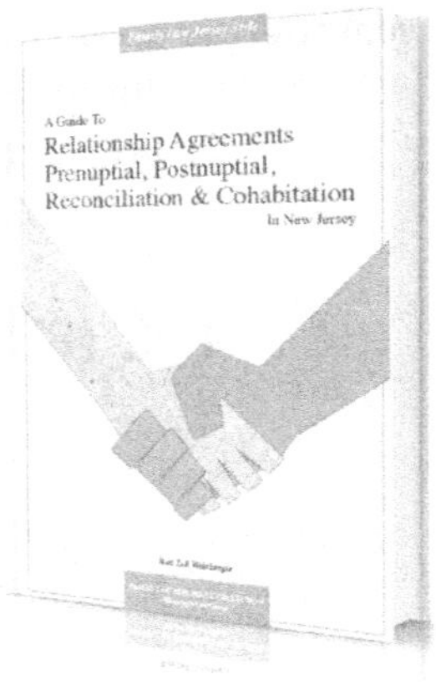

eBook versions of the Weinberger Law Group Library series can be ordered via Amazon or by visiting www.weinbergerlawgroup.com

Made in the USA
Monee, IL
04 November 2026

67387509R10059